# Praise for "When the Congregation is the Church"

*Rev. Dr. Lenworth Anglin thoughtfully interprets the biblical text in Acts of the Apostles 2:37 to 47. He pinpoints the problematic issue of blurring lines differentiating church from congregation by pastorally considering benchmarks of the Early Church in relation to right relationship with God, "one another" and the "community". Church leaders, pastors, seminarians will be provoked by engaging this timely book, including the areas for reflection and the appraisals.*

**Rev. Adinhair Jones**
Executive Chairman, Church of God in Jamaica
Pastor, Olson Memorial Church

*Rev Lenworth Anglin has been my colleague, friend and brother in Christ since childhood. Our theological and scholastic journeys have followed along similar paths, often intersecting in our various teaching assignments. I can truly say I know his mind and heart and his strong passion for the Church. He comes from a very strong and dynamic faith tradition, the Church of God Reformation Movement, which although not originating in the Caribbean, has been part of the Caribbean Church experience for more than a century. From his years of pastoral ministry in Jamaica, across the Caribbean, and in the UK, and his deep immersion and reflections in the Church of God Reformation Movement, he has produced this book as a guide to help those who have a genuine concern for the state of the Church in our nations today.*

*Pastor Lenworth Anglin has made a helpful distinction between a congregation and the church. He explains the difference in very clear and simple language. He traces the distinction in Scripture, particular in the book of Acts, and cites cogent examples of the difference. This book is a very helpful guide to those who desire a deeper experience of the 'true' Church. I therefore highly commend it to you.*

**Las G. Newman**, PhD, D. D. J.P.
Past President
Caribbean Graduate School of Theology

*"When the Congregation is the Church" is biblical, theological as well as practical. Being a careful student of the Bible by grounding his reflections on the Early Church, Lenworth Anglin masterfully illustrates how God, believers and community are wrapped up in ministry imperatives. This book should be read to deepen pastoral call and discipleship and strengthen scholarship.*

**Rev Courtney Gordon**
Chairman, Ministers' Conference
Church of God in Jamaica

*I was fortunate to witness the start of the Ministry of Reverend Doctor Lenworth Anglin when as young people we were part of the National Youth Council of the Church of God in Jamaica. From those early days he distinguished himself as not only an excellent preacher and teacher but as a mature leader who understood his role as Pastor. Rev Dr. Anglin's service is marked by a mature wisdom in dealing with Church relations as well as an ecumenical facilitator. After reading the first chapter of "When the Congregation is the Church," I was convinced of its relevance to the Church today. The book guides believers who wish to measure and evaluate their conduct as Christians but is also valuable for those who seek to have a wholesome lifestyle and to understand how faith in Jesus Christ makes this possible. I am happy that Rev. Dr. Anglin has written this book because his years of experience and practical counsel should be shared, and will provide guidance to the Church, its leaders and to people everywhere.*

**Mrs. Florence Holness Darby, O.D.**
Attorney-at-Law

# When the Congregation is the Church

# When the Congregation is the Church

## Reflections and Counsel for Church Effectiveness

### FOR PASTORS, CHURCH LEADERS, AND ASPIRING LEADERS

## Lenworth Newton Anglin, DMin, D.D.

Kingston, Jamaica W.I

Published by:
Extra MILE Innovators
4 Rochester Avenue,
Kingston 8, Jamaica W.I.
www.extramileja.com

Cover Design and Formatting: BambuSparks
www.bambusparks.com

Editing: Hyacinth Anglin




For bulk orders or feedback, contact the publisher at hyalen@yahoo.com.

*This book is dedicated to my wife and loyal supporter, Hyacinth Lenore Morris Anglin, without whom I could not have achieved this.*

# INTRODUCTION

My journey of giving pastoral care and oversight within the body of Christ began in earnest August 1973, when at a Summer Youth Camp of the Church of God in Jamaica[1], I answered the Call to full-time pastoral ministry. My own Pastoral ministry began long before the formal recognition by the Church in ordination. Shortly after that, I entered the Jamaica Theological Seminary (JTS) in the year 1974 with the intent of preparing for and solidifying the requirements of that Call. Indeed, I believe that my formal study, and training at the JTS, which I regard as vital, served to crystallize and develop the Call of God upon my life. This was later confirmed in 2006 while pursuing a Doctor of Ministry discipline at the Anderson School of Theology in Anderson, USA, where my convictions were strengthened and given further credibility.

---

[1] The "Church of God in Jamaica" is the recognized title used for the Church registered as "The Society of the Church of God in Jamaica". This body arose from the Church of God Reformation Movement, initiated in the early 1880s in the United States of America, which sent missionaries to the island in the year 1907 after the devastating earthquake of 1907. The missionaries who founded the Church of God in Jamaica were George and Nellie Olson, who came from Anderson, Indiana to Jamaica.

It is my strong belief that while all active members of the church are engaged in ministry on one level or another, fundamentally, there must be the Call to ministry and the understanding that it is God who calls us to our varying places of service/ministries. Over the years, in the various institutions where I have taught, I have emphasized that before a person selects the Christian Ministry, more so the Pastoral Ministry, he or she must have the assurance that the selection has been imperatively sanctioned by the covenant-keeping God. We must all be sure of the Divine Call and Commission, which I believe is never revoked.

Whatever the ministry is that one engages in, each person must approach it from a sound theological and biblical base. I submit that all ministry activities should address the current concerns that affect contemporary society. Therefore, it is important for each person to apply biblical principles to his or her everyday interaction with the population or community that he or she serves.

I believe that the God of the Christian community is the only true God. The creation account as described in the opening chapters of the book of Genesis informs me about the existence of the world and created order. A basic belief in the inspiration of Scriptures has been foundational to my own faith, and I believe in the authority of the Scriptures to the extent that, I regard anyone who rejects the authority of Scripture as not liberal but "lost." In the words of the writer to the Hebrews in chapter 11, faith in God begins with the acceptance that God is, and that He is the rewarder of them that diligently seek him.

The Bible is clear that all of humanity sinned in Adam (Romans 5:12-21), but the gift of God is eternal life through Jesus Christ (Romans 6:23). Jesus Christ, fully God and fully human was born of the Virgin Mary. He lived, served, and ultimately offered Himself as the full and final sacrifice for Sin. I believe in Jesus as the only Mediator between God and humankind, and that "neither is there salvation in any other, for there is no other name given among men whereby we must be saved" (Acts 4:12) I am persuaded also, as in the words of a favorite Church of God hymn

- "He Wants His Way in Thee" - that "God has sent the Holy Spirit to our hearts, an honored Guest, to deliver us from evil, and to bring us peace and rest."

The personal and second return of Jesus Christ will bring with it final rewards for the saints, as well as judgment for those who constantly reject the offer of salvation (2 Timothy 4:1 and 6-8). Experience does teach wisdom, and I have found that my theological understanding has become more cemented with experience. I also firmly believe that we serve the all-wise and infallible God, and that Romans 8: 28, is applicable and true, in declaring, *"All things do work together for good to those who love God, to those who are the called according to His purpose"*.

I am a fundamentalist in its traditional sense, but in my relationships with other religious groups, I have sought to be relevant, without compromise. The Church of God Reformation Movement, her doctrine, theology and practice influence my theological understanding significantly. Pioneer writers such as R. R. Byrum and D. S. Warner, along with classics such as "What the Bible Teaches" by F.G. Smith (with all the revisions) provide a constant platform for my faith and theology.

Additionally, the years during which I lived and served in the United Kingdom provided invaluable multi-cultural experience for me and my ministry. As part of a Theological Study Group of the Afro Caribbean Evangelical Alliance, my intellectual journey was made even more "colorful." Liberation Theology, and other similar schools of thought have surfaced as attractive alternatives, but I have maintained my position on orthodox theology, which has impacted my preaching, teachings, and writings over the years.

In 1992, I co-authored the book, "Let's Praise Him Again – an Afro-Caribbean Perspective on Worship." The preparation for, and publication of this work proved to be a priceless experience. I have also related to the thoughts of John Stott in his publications/writings on Christian involvement, James Cone in his "God of the Oppressed," and Richard Niebuhr 'Christ and Culture.' These writers have helped me along my journey by providing a broader view of soteriology and of God's work with and through humanity, class, and all cultures.

Over the years, the continuation of my journey allowed me to provide leadership in various capacities at a local and national level in Jamaica, the wider Caribbean, and the United Kingdom. I was one of the founders and leaders of the Jamaica Umbrella Groups of Churches and, for more than 20 years, I have been teaching a course on Church Leadership and Administration. It is against this background that I pen this book, designed to assist in providing guidance to pastors, leaders, and church members toward a more fulsome understanding of effective ministry and witness. In so doing, I am using the Early Church as a model, reflecting primarily on Acts chapter 2, and the lessons it teaches us about the church versus the congregation.

While my main sphere of ministry is dedicated to the Church of God Reformation Movement, I have related closely to a variety of denominations and church groups. Much of my reflections in this book are however, influenced by my beliefs framed and nurtured by the Church of God Reformation Movement. I have preached several sermons and taught many sessions on the theme *"When the Congregation is the Church."* This became my mantra, and is now my hallmark, flagship teaching and primary emphasis. This theme has indeed framed and shaped my ministry.

Drawing from several decades of ministry, this book reproduces some of the sermons I have taught on this subject and includes additional material for personal reflections and counsel. It highlights three characteristics that I posit may be used to define the church, and offers a distinction between Church and congregation with 'church' referring to the local church. It is my strong belief that the following characteristics differentiate the mere body of people coming together as a congregation at any event, from the Church, the Body of Christ:

(1) The people enjoy a right relationship with God

(2) The people enjoy a right relationship with each other

(3) The people enjoy a right relationship with the community
    that they serve.

I recognize the overlap evident in the above characteristics,
but the intention/focus is to demonstrate that each has its own
unique features.

This book will guide you in assessing the effectiveness of
your church in relation to both doctrine and practice. It also
challenges its readers to engage in deep introspection of all the
tenets set forth. To this end, two assessment instruments have
been included as Appendices, designed to encourage the
leadership of any congregation or church in assessing and/or
appraising each body of believers over which God has called
such leaders to be overseers. This author's intention is that each
leader will perform such examination considering the examples
of the Early Church in Acts 2: 37-47. Since this is also applicable
to individuals, each reader is also encouraged to engage in self-
appraisal and assessment of his or her own ministry values.

This book is not intended to give a broad spectrum of church
polity and practice. It will not provide leadership skills and
advice for the administration and management of the church. It
however points the readers' attention to the biblical reference in
the book of Acts where the Early Church is modelled,
highlighting specific characteristics that must identify the church.
The emphasis is on the examples established then by the early
disciples; examples which are still relevant and required today,
as the congregation becomes the church.

When the congregation is the church, the distinguishing
feature is that the assembly is comprised of persons who have
experienced faith in God and salvation through faith in Jesus
Christ, aided by the Holy Spirit. This understanding will guide
their lifestyle and influence their conduct. When the congregation
is the church, the Bible is the standard guide for living the
regenerated life, in every sphere of existence. When the
congregation is the church, the people enjoy a right relationship
with God. When the congregation is the church, the people enjoy

a right relationship with each other. When the congregation is the church, the people enjoy a right relationship with the community that they serve.

# Contents

# PART 1

# THE PEOPLE ENJOY A RIGHT RELATIONSHIP WITH GOD

# CHAPTER 1

# CHURCH OR CONGREGATION?

Early in my ministry I was approached by a young woman who was faithfully attending morning worship services each week with the congregation with which she was affiliated. She admitted that, raised in a devout family, she was sincerely going through the motions of attending church and following the requirements as she understood them to be. Although intellectually brilliant, and having a fear of God, she did not know about the plan of salvation through faith in Jesus Christ. She admitted that if asked she would say that she was a Christian.

However, one day she was invited by a colleague to attend his church. It was there the gospel message was preached to her, the invitation was made, and she responded to the call of God upon her life. It was a change; it was a revelation; it was a new beginning. It was only then that she identified with the church. Therefore, although she was in congregation, in the gathering of the "faithful" people, she was not in church. This may well be the case with many other persons, who sincerely gather in congregations, without a clear biblical understanding and knowledge of salvation or what becoming a part of the Church really means.

This book makes the distinction between the congregation, which is the assembly of persons, and the church, which is God's "called out ones". For our purposes, the question naturally arises as to what is the congregation? I will treat with some of the steps or characteristics that I believe will identify the church, and distinguish it from the congregation, by using the scripture passage in the second chapter of Acts.

## What is a Congregation?

Wikipedia offers several definitions of the word 'congregation'. A congregation may be merely a gathering or collection of people, animals, or things. The word also refers to an assembly, flock, pack, group, herd, body, crowd, company, or multitude.

This definition also includes followers, adherents, and even a mob.

Spectators at a sports event comprise a congregation. Reunions at a family get-together are a congregation. A congregation in its broader sense, therefore, does not necessarily mean a church or the Church. I contend that it is possible to have a gathering of persons, which is a congregation but is not necessarily the Church.

# What or Who is the Church?

The Church consists of those who have appropriated the gift of salvation. They are the "called out" ones. It is God who ultimately determines who belongs in the membership of the church, but it is important that humanly visible methods be employed to recognize this fact. Baptism is an outward manifestation of the inward change but does not determine membership. Church may therefore be understood as local and visible, as well as universal and invisible.

The nearest idea to a church concept was that of the family, as seen in the earliest chapters of the Bible. In the earliest Old Testament families, the father acted as the priest and leader (seen in Adam and Noah), and later the role of father expanded to that of patriarch (as seen in Abraham, Isaac, Jacob and his twelve sons). Under Moses, religious life changed, and a theocracy (the rule of God) emerged. In that theocracy, God was the Chief Ruler, Priest, King, and Prophet, and He established His law, His tabernacle, and His temple. Perhaps the best term to describe such persons who worshipped and obeyed God during that period is simply the 'People of God.'

In the New Testament, the concept of Church is definitely developed. The term *ekklesia* is used to describe an organized group of persons whose intent is to worship and obey God. The Church is more than a single denomination. The Church is not an improved Judaism. The Church represents the saved of all ages. The Church therefore exists in two contexts in the Bible. First, in the universal sense, the Church is all who have been reborn of God and baptized into the Body of Christ. Secondly, in the local sense, the Church includes those in the universal church who have linked themselves together into a specific community.

The Church of God Reformation Movement pioneer, Russell R. Byrum presents some definitions of the church, which I consider to be authentic. These definitions have guided my understanding of the Church and are always relevant. Byrum propounds that "the term "universal church" in its broadest sense, is used of the entire company of those whom God has called in all ages whether they be on earth or in heaven. It consists of the aggregate of those who have been regenerated."

Byrum also defines the local church as follows:

The local church is the local embodiment and exhibition of the universal church. It is the company of the regenerate persons of a given community associated together according to the Scriptures for worship and the upbuilding of the kingdom of God. It is not merely an association of persons who have joined themselves together for social, benevolent, or even a religious purpose.[2]

I therefore propose that the true local church is a divine organization. It is composed of all persons who have accepted salvation through faith in Jesus Christ, who all have the same Spirit, and who are all joined to the living "Head of the body." This understanding becomes a lived experience when members of a congregation and of the Church recognize the unifying element of this relationship, that the Church is one Body.

---

[2] Russell R. Byrum, *Christian Theology: A Systematic Statement of Christian Doctrine for the Use of Theological Students.* (Anderson, IN: Gospel Trumpet Company, 1925), 508.

As mentioned earlier, the foundation for this book is based on Acts, chapter 2 verses 37 through 47, which reads as follows:

[37]Now when they heard this, they were pricked in their heart, and said unto Peter and to the rest of the apostles, Men and brethren, what shall we do? [38]Then Peter said unto them, Repent, and be baptized every one of you in the name of Jesus Christ for the remission of sins, and ye shall receive the gift of the Holy Ghost. [39]For the promise is unto you, and to your children, and to all that are afar off, *even* as many as the Lord our God shall call. [40]And with many other words did he testify and exhort, saying, Save yourselves from this untoward generation. [41]Then they that gladly received his word were baptized: and the same day there were added *unto them* about three thousand souls. [42]And they continued steadfastly in the apostles' doctrine and fellowship, and in breaking of bread, and in prayers. [43]And fear came upon every soul: and many wonders and signs were done by the apostles. [44]And all that believed were together, and had all things common; [45]And sold their possessions and goods, and parted them to all *men*, as every man had need. [46]And they, continuing daily with one accord in the temple, and breaking bread from house to house, did eat their meat with gladness and singleness of heart, [47]Praising God, and having favor with all the people. And the Lord added to the church daily such as should be saved (KJV).

The Early Church as described in this passage will be used as a model for describing the authentic Church and is applicable to any period or age. As a note of caution, readers must understand that The Early Church did not demonstrate 100% perfection. In Acts chapter five, we find deceit and sin with Ananias and Sapphira. In Acts chapter six, there arose a murmuring of the Grecians against the Hebrews because their widows were neglected in the daily ministration. Indeed, in the Early Church, the negatives were not ignored; they were addressed under God, (by the leading of the Holy Spirit, and the church leaders). In this way, the Church grew strong and thrived. I therefore, believe that as local churches we must always:

- Be objective in our analyses

- Ensure that the few negative situations do not overshadow the many positive ones.

# Reflection

As you reflect on the issues raised, look again at the examples of the negatives in Acts chapters 5 and 6. These did not hinder the growth of the church and the spread of the gospel. In Acts chapter 5, although Ananias and Sapphira lied and cheated, the ministry of the Early Church continued. The gospel records show that the church continued a powerful ministry with signs and wonders. Believers were added to the Lord, and there was church growth.

In Acts chapter 6, the quarrel over the widows being neglected was such that the people murmured. The situation was resolved, and the work of God increased. We serve the Positive God who works, and who accomplishes His purpose in spite of human failings. Assess your situation: are you a member of a congregation or a member of the Church?

# CHAPTER 2

# FROM CONGREGATION TO CHURCH

In making the transition from a mere congregation of people to becoming the Church, the congregants must display the signal distinction of enjoying ***the right relationship with God.*** This is crucial. This is vital. A personal, intimate connection with the Deity is the initial step in forging a right relationship with God. I will treat in this chapter with some of the specific characteristics or elements that must identify the Church, and the members of the Church. Consider the descriptions laid out in the foundation text.

## The Conviction

In the verses leading up to verse 37 of our passage, the Bible identifies Conviction as that they were first pricked in their hearts as Peter declared the Gospel of Jesus Christ. Upon the conviction by the Holy Spirit, they were then moved to ask what they needed to do next. This indicated that they followed up on the first quickening of the emotions they experienced as stirred by the Holy Spirit. They acknowledged the quickening, responded, then decided to commit to the call.

Many individuals, then and now, are pricked in their hearts, yet go their various ways emoted but not decided. They make no decision to accept the invitation of a Holy God desiring to engage in personal communion with humankind. The example set forth by the Early Church is that they acknowledged their conviction, and took decisive action, which led to their conversion experience. This conversion was shown by their changed lives.

Conviction can be an instantaneous or a gradual experience. This depends upon each situation. One night, while preaching at an open-air meeting in a troubled community, I sensed the evidence of great conviction upon the hearts of many. There was a spontaneous reaction to the gospel by a hardened criminal, who, with tears, delivered his gun to me. He confessed that he was on his way to commit a murder but heard the message, was convicted, acted on that conviction, and made a decision to turn over his life to God. It must be noted here that the appropriate follow-up actions were taken after that meeting, in accordance with the legal requirements.

# The Explanation

In addition to the conviction that the hearers experience, the next step in the process ought to be the explanation of what is happening. As shown in Acts 2:38 through 40, Peter explained to the seekers God's prophetic promise and the way of restoration to God. It is critical that an explanation of the message of the good news of Jesus Christ be explained in simple terms so that the hearers not only hear, but also understand the message. This is crucial. It is not left to emotional outbursts at the time when the hearts are pricked with conviction. It is directed at the intellect of the hearers. It seeks to confirm the conviction. Just as Peter was able to refer to the prophecy in the book of Joel – "this is that" – we must ensure that we use Biblical references, in our declaration of the gospel. It is imperative that the Scripture explains Who Jesus is, why we preach Him, and what our response to this message should be.

# The Response to the Gospel

***They were obedient to the Gospel preached [v 41].*** In the model church being used for this book the people listened, they heard; they responded. Whatever interpretation we apply to Peter's declaration in verses 38 through 40, it is clear from Scripture that the declaration of the Gospel requires a response. (See John 3 verses 14 to 21.) In the case of our text under consideration, the response was positive. They were obedient. They gladly received the word. They acted upon it by willingly joining in with the group. This act of the individual's will is the intrinsic key to accepting, believing and committing one's life to the Way. It is to be a conscious decision on the part of the individual.

# The Baptism and Holy Communion

They appropriated the message that was declared and *were baptized* (v 41). Reference to Baptism raises many discussion points including the broader issue of ordinances and sacraments. I will approach the subject with a heavy influence of the viewpoint of the Church of God Reformation Movement. It will be important, also, to include the Holy Communion in this treatment, as we believe it is one of the ordinances.

The study of our model church in this work would be incomplete without the observances of the ordinances of the Lord. An ordinance is defined as a symbolic or representational observance with the emphasis placed on God and His work in the life of the individual. In contrast to the reference of the observance as a sacrament, the ordinances require no priestly mediation. The sacraments tend to place the emphasis on the ritual, and stress that grace is conferred directly.

In our text under consideration, it is clear that the Early Church members observed both the ***Baptism and the Breaking of Bread***. These are the Baptism, and the Lord's Supper or Holy Communion. Although the reference to *'breaking of bread'* in verse 47 is unclear, I believe it refers to the Holy Communion.

It is also important to clarify here that the Church of God Reformation Movement regards three events as ordinances: the Baptism, Holy Communion and Foot-washing. These ordinances are emphasized to enable the members' understanding of the doctrine, to teach them the practices, and to celebrate the command of Christ. The ordinance is an affirmation of our beliefs, and serves as a testimony of the believer's commitment. The Church of God Reformation Movement observes these three ordinances because they were practiced by Christ during His earthly ministry. He commanded or instructed the church to practice them, and the Early Church practiced.

Foot-washing is taught as an expression of Christian service and love. It is a service that emphasizes humbleness, not humiliation, and is generally observed on the evening of Holy

Thursday during Holy Week. For the purposes of this book, I did not conduct research on the current practice of the Foot-washing ceremony within the Jamaican churches. It is not included since the passage of Scripture used for this book refers only to the Baptism and the Breaking of Bread.

# The Doctrine

Having joined or agreed to take up membership with a local body of believers, the converts are encouraged to attend to the teachings or doctrines of the group or denomination with which they are now associated. In the Early Church, the members engaged in the study of the Word and teachings of the apostles [v 42]. Our model church presents us with a picture of adherents who faithfully attended the teachings organized by their leaders. They studied the apostles' doctrine. They pored over the scriptures, the prophecies, and the current messages regarding the Messiah. In today's local church, this ministry is normally managed likewise through regular weekly study programs geared to enhancing the spiritual maturity and growth of each believer. No church can exist without this segment of ministry to its converts. There will be no spiritual growth or maturity without this. Leaders therefore ought to take heed of this very necessary assignment. It is vital that Bible study classes be given high priority among the various other activities that are placed on the agenda of the local church. By extension, this also requires that the leaders themselves adequately and accurately prepare to teach the correct doctrine to the congregation and the Church.

# The Fellowship

The Early Church highly regarded fellowship as an integral component of meetings. The believers ***continued steadfastly in fellowship*** (v 42) with spiritual maturity resulting. An important word to note is, "steadfastly". This connotes a commitment borne out of the earnest desire to learn more of the Lord and His word. As it was then for the Early Church, so it ought to be today for all local churches. Fellowship enables the 'babe' in Christ to adopt and adapt to the ways of the Christian living and principles. This kind of fellowship fosters rapid growth and provides a deeper, more meaningful understanding of the needs of others among the Body of believers. This writer will not prescribe the various fellowship opportunities to be utilized by a given church, except to state that the infants and youths ought not to be neglected. Leaders must endeavor to be inclusive in fellowship. When fellowship activities are organized, they will lead to the right interpersonal relationships between church groups and with each other. This will eventually result in the family bonding, caring, and sharing to be discussed in the following chapter, as we continue to look at the model church.

# The Prayer Meetings

The Early Church, as our model, emphasized the need for prayer. According to the scripture passage in Acts chapter 2, the believers ***continued steadfastly in prayers (v 42).*** Enough cannot be stressed regarding the need to learn how to pray; to know what to pray for; to know when to pray; or how to exercise one's prayer muscles to achieve the needful outcomes of a spirit-filled life. These aspects of prayer are themselves a complete study that each congregation or church body should diligently embark upon and emphasize. Though not the focus of this book, let us not forget that fasting is often linked with prayer, and is highly endorsed by other scriptures. It therefore becomes important to speak to this at this point.

Matthew 4 verses 1 to 11 provide us with the example of Jesus, who Himself took time out to go aside into the wilderness to fast. Despite the fact that there are many views on fasting, it has been a priority in my life and ministry. Prayer and Fasting are components of the Right Relationship with God, as shown in our model church, and in numerous instances, the supernatural element manifested.

# The Supernatural Element

The members of the Early Church in the text under consideration for this publication submitted themselves as instruments in God's Hand for the working of miracles *"many wonders and signs"* (v 43). It is my deep conviction that the people of God, the Church, the "called out ones" should demonstrate the wonders and signs promised by Jesus Himself. My strong position with regard to the modern day miracle is influenced by the question: *What exactly is a miracle?*

The working of miracles is a spiritual gift in which the person exercising the gift invokes the miraculous intervention of God to a given situation with the result that God receives recognition for the supernatural intervention. (See 1 Corinthians 12:10). I believe sincerely that everything ABOUT God is a miracle. In fact, Our God can do anything in any way, at any time He wills to do so. He is the Omnipotent One! God can therefore choose to bypass what to us are natural means to accomplish what He wants to do, when, or if He wills. He has a long-standing reputation of defying the very laws of nature to deliver or heal his people.

Healing, for example, gets its source from God and has its source in God, and God alone. The spiritual gift of healing refers to the supernatural ability to heal people of physical diseases in response to a laying on of hands, or praying, or commanding to be healed or some combination of them by the person having the gift. (See 1 Corinthians 12:9). Doctors and other medical personnel are agents of healing, but God very often bypasses them and their efforts, performing the miraculous, by His own means, simply because He can.

Let me introduce my personal experience with the supernatural intervention of God to effect healing upon my body. This occurred in June 1981 when the medical expectation was that I would have died within months. The church was called to a time of prayer and fasting on my account. I was visited by two of my pastoral colleagues, who, although not allowed entry into my hospital room, stood outside the door, and prayed the prayer of healing.

The medical specialist informed me of the recommended intervention, but I refused to accept this on the basis that I knew I had received a divine touch. The words of that specialist still echo in my memory: "Doctors recommend; patients decide". I asked him if he had heard of Jesus. I then told him I was healed and asked to be discharged from the hospital. The healing of that condition was a direct supernatural intervention by God, and it has never returned. Praise the Lord!

With regard to the display of the supernatural by the Church, there are theological views that such manifestations were only needed as confirmation of the gospel during the apostolic age, as exemplified in the book of Acts chapter 8, only at special times, and are no longer applicable. It is further suggested in certain circles that this confirmation is no longer required or necessary.

In response to that position, it is my firm, unwavering conviction that the supernatural outworking and display of spiritual gifts are still active, present, alive, and available today and are needed now, even more than ever, in the church. These are needed as confirmation for at least two reasons. Firstly, there is clear, strong unbelief that exists in the world. Agnosticism abounds and Atheism is rampant. Secondly, there is clear demonstration of demonic forces at work in the world and it is only the supernatural power of God that can deal with both reasons. Along with the supernatural power of God is the manifested, experienced power of praise and worship bringing a new dimension of worship where God Himself inhabits the praises of His people (Psalm 22:3).

# Praises and Worship

The model church fellowshipped with joy, praising God daily in unity with one another [v 47]. Without praise, the assembly is meaningless. Without praise, the meeting is listless. Without praise, the Object of the praise is not invited to be present in the midst of the congregation.

There has been a great deal of talks, discussions, and even arguments about Praise and Worship. I am, however, mindful of the fact that this was not an issue with the Early Church according to the passage under review. Let us examine some relevant points on worship as we consider the matter of praise.

# The Meaning of Worship

The Oxford Dictionary defines worship as 'to honour and revere a supernatural being, to adore with appropriate acts, rites and ceremonies'. The New Bible Dictionary states that the essential concept of worship in both the Old and New Testaments is *service*. The Hebrew word used to denote worship is *aboda*, a word whose root is drawn from the labour of slaves and hired servants, and which carries the overtones of service specifically to Jehovah. Israel's worship of Jehovah focused on the God of Abraham, Isaac and Jacob. Their faith was monotheistic (a belief in one God) and could not therefore accommodate the worship of any other deity. This principle was enshrined in the Hebrew law 'Thou shalt worship no other god' (Exodus 34:14). In the Old Testament, Judgement was instantaneous for the disobedient (See Deuteronomy 8:19; 11:16-17; 30:17-18).

In the New Testament, several Greek words are used to refer to worship. The most frequent of these are *proskuneo, sebamai, sebazomai, latrueo, eusebeo,* and *therapueo*. The Greek word *proskuneo* is used widely in the Gospels, Acts, and the Apocrypha. Only once is it used in the Pauline epistles (1 Corinthians 14:25), and its original meaning stems from two

Greek words *pros* (towards) and *kuneo* (to kiss). *Proskuneo* thus expresses the idea of kissing the hand in homage, to make obeisance, or to bow down in surrender.

*Sebamai* and *sebazomai* concentrate on the underlying attitude of reverence, to feelings of awe and devotion. The emphasis is placed on the overriding presence of God in our midst. *Latrueo* is used in a similar way to *proskuneo*, to give homage, but with the added emphasis of service intrinsic in its usage (See Philippians 3:3). *Eusebeo* links worship to pious acts. In Acts 17:23 Paul uses it in relation to the Athenians' objects of worship. This word takes in the element of ritualistic observance.

*Therapueo* denotes the healing process that worship engenders. Worship and healing come together through a washing of our being as we approach God. This word throws light on the fact that the Jewish priesthood went through several ceremonial washings before coming to God. Even as we praise, healing properties are released into us body and soul. Our vision expands, our inner beings are strengthened, and our spirits are liberated to worship beyond earthly limitations.

# Corporate Worship in the Bible

The Old Testament clearly shows the centrality of the worship of Jahweh, the God of Israel, in national life, yet it hardly provides us with any full description of one such act of worship, whether an isolated sacrifice or a major festival in Jerusalem. Some special orders of service are described, such as Solomon's dedication of the temple (2 Chronicles 5 – 7), and certain stipulations about the way in which sacrifices should be offered are given (Leviticus chapters 6 to 7), but we do not see the whole picture with spoken liturgy, ceremonial action, and detailed rubrics all included.

The New Testament also says little about the form and content of worship in the local church, though such passages as Acts 2, Acts 20, 1 Corinthians 12 – 14, and 1 Thessalonians 5 v

16 do provide us with an idea of the order of service followed in the Early Church.

So why do we worship?

- We have been commanded to worship God – Exodus 20: 2-3 and 34:14.
- It takes the focus off us, directing it to God, and acknowledging that He is the Sovereign Lord of the universe.
- Worship prepares us to receive God's Word. If we practice a life of worship, we are listening carefully to God.
- The practice of worship provides us the opportunity to look at all of life through the lenses of worship.

So, as we focus on God, shifting our attention away from ourselves and our circumstances, focusing instead on His Word, we will begin to see the rest of life as God sees it – as it really is. The more we express our adoration of God in worship, the more distinctly we can view our lives from His perspective.

In the New Testament the disciples sang in the Upper Room (Mark 14:26). Paul instructed believers to sing psalms, hymns and spiritual songs (Ephesians 5:18 -20). He and Silas sang praises in prison at midnight (Acts 16:25). That the redeemed will sing in heaven is foretold in Revelation 15:3.

# Reflection

I encourage you, the reader, to pause now, and consider your own relationship with God. How well do you measure up against the example of the model church? Examine the two two-paged appraisal instruments (Appendix 1 and Appendix 2), developed to assist you in your reflection. Both appraisal forms are geared towards assessment of the same characteristics presented in reference to the church. With regard to the right relationship with God, consider your own experience at the time of your conviction to follow Christ. Consider also, the explanation you received pertaining to the Gospel message. How clear was it? Was there any follow-up to your repentance? As a leader, examine how you handle the conviction experience of new believers and how you explain the Gospel message. How clearly do you present the Gospel message? Is there follow-up to repentance? What about your congregation? Is the doctrine being disseminated in regular Bible studies? What about the ordinances? Baptism, Holy Communion, are they being observed faithfully? As you read further, I exhort you to contemplate the issues on an individual level, as well as to assess your own congregation. Is it looking like the church? Or is it a mere congregation?

# PART 2

# THE PEOPLE ENJOY A RIGHT RELATIONSHIP WITH EACH OTHER

# CHAPTER 3

# WHEN RELATIONSHIPS ARE RIGHT IN CHURCH

In reference again to the selected passage in the Book of Acts, I believe that the model church describes the fact that *the people enjoyed a right relationship with each other.* Coupled with this is the fact that the people displayed true *recognition of the leadership.* Clearly defined and respected leadership offices were evident in the Early Church. The apostles' doctrine, mentioned in verse 42 of our study, carries the ring of respect for leadership in all its aspects.

As I reflect on my many years of ministry, I recall instances when our church fellowship was enhanced by my leading social activities outside of the chapel walls. One such activity was the family sports day, when old and young participated in games and athletics, including even a cricket match that we held on the grounds of our high school. It was a blessing to see a foot race for women being won by the oldest female deacon. In leading the charge, I batted for the younger team in cricket, and was subsequently bowled out by an older evangelist. I remember also my taking a church trip to the beach, when members confessed that they had never before been to the seaside in their lives. Yet, such activities did not deter them from following my leadership in true fellowship and love. Those were days of bonding which fostered *koinonia* in the local church and among the members, who willingly and eagerly followed their pastor. This was also good for me, as I was a younger man leading a large membership of older persons, who demonstrated their respect for the leadership I provided.

## The Recognition of the Leadership

The issue of Clergy versus Laity becomes important at this point, as it has caused major discussions and much division within Christendom. The main feature of this issue surrounds the understanding of the Church as the Body of Christ. There are two positions related to this issue, inciting contention: 1. That the Church as the Body of Christ means the whole body of believers functions together as equals but are different in roles and abilities.

2.  The opposing view that the Church, as the Body of Christ, means the whole Body functions with hierarchical divisions and distinctions that matter.  The doctrine of the priesthood of the believers teaches however, that all members of the church function together to carry out the ministry of the church and that all members are equal but function differently.

The supporters of the opposing view that all members are not equals in ministry, contend that some have been called to the ministry, distinctly and separately from the rest of the church. This results in the distinction between Clergy and Laity. The Clergy consists of those persons called and ordained to Christian ministry, while the others without such a call and ordination are referred to as Laity. Both positions appeal to the Bible for substantiation, and both have historical precedence and practice.

I am conscious and aware of the presenting conflicts found in an analysis of the doctrine of the priesthood of all believers. It is my belief that the Bible's teaching on the role of leadership, spiritual gifts, and the place of work and vocation, would clarify the ministry of the church. It is important therefore to examine the various passages that relate to these areas, and to arrive at a central teaching.

R. Paul Stevens in his book, "The Other Six Days: Vocation, Work, and Ministry in Biblical Perspectives", states emphatically the Biblical basis for the doctrine. He states that we look in vain in the New Testament for a theology of the Laity. There are neither laypersons nor clergy. The word 'laypersons' (*laikoi*) was first used by Clement of Rome at the end of the first century, but was never used by an inspired apostle in Scripture to describe second-class, untrained and unequipped Christians. That word ought to be eliminated from our vocabulary. 'Laity", in its proper New Testament sense of *laos* – the people of God - is a term of great honor denoting the enormous privilege and mission of the whole people of God. Once we were not a people at all, but now in Christ, we are 'a chosen people, a royal priesthood, a holy nation, a people [*laos*] belonging to God' (1 Peter 2:9; Exodus 19:6).

The word 'clergy' comes from the Greek word *klēros*, which means the 'appointed or endowed' ones. It is used in Scripture not for the leaders of the people but for the **whole** people. Ironically the church in its constitution is a people without laity in the usual sense of that word, but full of clergy in the true sense of that word – endowed, commissioned and appointed by God to continue God's own service and mission in the world. So, the church does not 'have' a minister; it is ministry, God's *ministerium*. It does not 'have' a mission; it is mission. There is one people, one Trinitarian people, one people that reflects the one God who is lover, beloved and love itself, as Augustine once said, and one God who is sender, sent and sending.[3]

In appealing to the Old Testament, one could make the point that there is continuity between the Testaments concerning the requirements for the people of God, yet there is radical discontinuity in the understanding of the role of the leader. The passage in Exodus chapter 28 verse 1 through chapter 30 verse 10 rightly describes what obtained under the old covenant ministry with a priestly caste and tribe, and the sacerdotal mediation of the priests, although in Exodus 19 verse 6 there is reference to God's people as priests.

In the New Testament, there is the teaching that each individual in his or her own right can now boldly approach God, the Most High without the need for the human priestly mediator between God and man. Yet, in terms of the leadership, the passage of Scripture in Ephesians 4:11-12 teaches that God has uniquely equipped some of the priestly servants (as described in 1 Peter 2:9-10) to train others in how to serve. In addition, Romans 12:1, 2 describe the Christian's life as a total priesthood. In the new covenant ministry, all believers are favored with unlimited experiences of power, sovereignty and the rule of Christ in their lives. (Mark 1:15 and Ephesians 1:19-22).

---

[3] R. Paul Stevens, *The Other Six Days: Vocation, Work, and Ministry in Biblical Perspectives* (Grand Rapids, MI: Wm. B. Eerdmans Publishing Company, 2000), 5.

The text of Scripture found in 1 Peter 2:9-10 provides for me a clear treatment of the subject. This epistle was addressed to the entire church. In fact, the titles used in this passage are all corporate. There the church is described as a royal priesthood. In the New Testament, the characteristic term is *diakonia*, which appears only in the Book of Esther among the Old Testament books. However, it is not used there to refer to any priestly function.

The change in language from Old to New Testaments implies a change also in doctrine, since ministry in the New Testament sense is not the exclusive privilege of a priestly caste. The word *leitourgia* is retained to describe the work of the Jewish priesthood (Luke 1:23; Hebrews 9:21), and it is applied, also, to the more excellent ministry of Christ (Hebrews 8:6). It can also be furthermore applied in a metaphorical sense to the spiritual service rendered by prophets and preachers of the Gospel (Acts 13:2; Romans 15:16). It remains true in general however, that the New Testament uses priestly language only in reference to the body of believers as a whole (Philippians 2:17; 1 Peter 2:9).

The historical change in the types and formats of Christian ministry demonstrates several movements towards church renewal over the last generation. Some of these renewals have changed our understanding of the Christian life, of ministry and of the character of the Church. For example:

- The Charismatic Movement
- Small Groups Movement
- Worship Renewal Movement
- Spiritual Gifts Movement
- Ecumenical Movement
- Church Growth Movement
- Seeker Church Movement, and
- The New Paradigm Church Movement.

They all, in one way or the other, forced the church to re-evaluate how we do ministry, and how we operate in the Body of Christ. I would like to add to this list "The Church of God Reformation Movement" with which I am associated and involved. This Movement is a reaction to sectarianism as it obtained in the 1880s in the United States of America. The message of this Movement spread to several other countries including Jamaica, in the year 1907.

The book of Acts, in addition to serving as an historical document, gives insight into God's provision and standard for the Church. The leaders especially in Acts 4:32 through 9:31 were focused on fulfilling their role in the overall ministry of the Church. In Acts 20:28 Paul admonishes leaders to feed the Church of God. The leaders are described as overseers. Their function is to feed and equip the Church. This is consistent with Ephesians 4:11-12 where the fact highlighted is that leaders are identified by function more so than by position and hierarchy. In Acts 6, the apostles clearly understood their role and sought the corporate response of the entire body in making decisions, thereby exemplifying structure in the Body of Christ.

The doctrine of the priesthood of believers does not contradict structure. There is need for senior pastor or an individual, or individuals who are ultimately responsible. This doctrine acknowledges and supports recognized leadership. However, let me introduce the need for support for the recognized leadership of the Church. The Apostle Paul encourages this support in his epistle to the believers in Thessalonica, when he writes in 1 Thessalonians 5: 12-13:

> [12] And we beseech you, brethren, to know them which labour among you, and are over you in the Lord, and admonish you; [13] And to esteem them very highly in love for their work's sake. And be at peace among yourselves.

He also states a principle of stewardship in the passage of scripture found in 1 Timothy chapter 5 verses 17 to 18 as follows:

> [17]Let the elders that rule well be counted worthy of double honour, especially they who labour in the word and doctrine. [18]For the scripture saith, Thou shalt not muzzle the ox that treadeth out the corn. And, The labourer is worthy of his reward.

These examples involved the recognition of the leadership, and the appropriate financial compensation and or support.

Spiritual gifts as described in 1 Corinthians chapters 12 and 14, Romans chapter 12, 1 Peter chapter 4, and Ephesians chapter 4 are sovereignly by God given to every member of the Church, so that the church may grow quantitatively and qualitatively. The very zeal, which a dedicated Christian has for the Kingdom's work may be a source of embarrassment and annoyance, unless that member is given guidance, and is instructed in achieving and maintaining harmony with others. The church has a 'corporateness' which is in itself a witness. Internal harmony is essential to that witness. Those in leadership are given the responsibility to speak the truth in love and to offer ministry in humility so that the church might grow up into Christ. The objective of the true leader is to produce a body of people who are individually and corporately responsive to Christ in what He is doing in the Church, through the Church, and throughout the world.

It therefore means that each member of the local church is part of the Universal Church on mission. Scripture passages such as Genesis chapters 1 and 2, and Colossians 3:17 teach that work is sacred, and that whatever we do, we must seek to glorify God. Vocation in the Christian believer's life is Christian, sacred and spiritual. The distinction that the Bible makes is between 'sacred' and 'sinful', not between 'sacred' and 'secular'. The local church then seeks to fulfill the mandate described in 1 Peter 2:9, 10 and 2 Corinthians chapter 4 to "show forth the praises of Him who brought us out of darkness into His marvelous light", exemplifying the right relationships with each other.

# The Caring and Sharing

Having the ***right relationship with each other*** in the body is evidenced, also, by the level of caring and sharing that exists. In describing the model church, our text states that they shared all things generously with the believers in their need - ***had all things common*** (verses 44 – 46). It is my understanding that this includes ensuring that no member experiences lack in any way and of any nature. To share all things common is to demonstrate 'agape' love (sincere, unconditional love) and engage in fellowship that in turn strengthens the love of each believer, thereby creating a confident atmosphere of genuine care. It is treating each other exactly as you would want to be treated. "Therefore, all things whatsoever ye would that men should do to you, do ye even so to them: for this is the law and the prophets". Matthew 7:12. Reference to this agape kind of love comes also from the New Testament passage in 1 Corinthians chapter 13, commonly referred to as the "Love Chapter. Chapter 4 of this book will elaborate on this love, which is the kind of love that fuels Oneness and Unity in relationships.

# The Oneness / Unity

The type of "Oneness" we preach is also expressed in the Scripture. ***They continued daily with one accord*** [v 46]. The apostles in the Early Church had come from different family backgrounds and various locations across Palestine. They had not all known each other before. Some were blood relatives, but it was through their association with Jesus that they all met each other.

It must be noted that though all were associated with Jesus, the members of our model church had different personalities. Even after living daily in the presence and influence of Jesus, their personality traits never changed! These early members were also at different academic and intelligence levels. We could also add to the list of differences that may have existed among them. Yet, ***they were all with one accord in one place.*** (Acts 2 v 1). That concept is mind-blowing! They were one in that they all met Jesus. They all followed Jesus, and by the time of the Upper Room experience, they were all one in obedience to the final instructions of Jesus.

What does the apostle Paul say about this "Oneness"? He especially stresses that the Church, though made up of many individuals, is essentially united (1 Corinthians 12). He bases that unity on the foundation of the "apostles and prophets" as well as on the cornerstone which is Christ (Ephesians 2:19-22). So strongly does Paul promote the unity of the church that he identifies it with Christ (1 Corinthians 12 v 27) - just as Christ cannot be divided, so the church must not be divided even though it is composed of many members.

Although the aim is for mutual respect for the doctrinal position of each member group or denomination, I have had to contend with the traditional position of the Church of God Reformation Movement in Jamaica regarding ***church unity***. This is one of the major tenets of the Movement. The Church of God in Jamaica is not a member of any umbrella group in its strictest definition but receives and retains full recognition as an umbrella group.

The umbrella groups in Jamaica are the various church associations comprising individual church denominations, such as the Jamaica Council of Churches, Jamaica Union Conference of Seventh Day Adventists, Jamaica Pentecostal Union (Apostolic), Jamaica Association of Full Gospel Churches, Jamaica Association of Evangelicals, and The Independent Churches of Jamaica. These umbrella groups represent the Church in the island.

The influence of the Church of God in Jamaica has been so pronounced that this recognition as an umbrella group has been achieved. My own recognition and influence as a church leader in Jamaica is also a proven advantage as I was then Executive

Chairman of the Church of God in Jamaica. . All of this is against the background of the concerns of the pioneers of the Church of God Reformation Movement. There is a standard of so-called unity made prominent throughout Christendom, which is simply an attempt to bring together the professed followers of Christ by external organization. This may be in the form of human denominational organization, or in the grouping together of a number of such individual organizations, but such can never be more than a counterfeit. True unity is of the heart, and it can be effected only by meeting Bible conditions. We believe that bringing together multitudes of people, the majority of whom know nothing about a saved experience and sinless life, and never have been born again – is not in any sense an exhibition of true Bible unity. Bible unity is based on spiritual life and is in accordance with the Word and Spirit of God.

# Reflection

In pausing for reflection, you, the reader should examine yourself as an individual first then as a leader (if you are one in your local church). Evaluate yourself in respect of the right relationships with each other. Consider your interpersonal relationships. How do you measure up? How does your church measure up? Please be prayerful as you meditate on the issues raised. Use the appraisal forms in the appendices that were developed for you.

# CHAPTER 4

# THOUGHTS OF LOVE
# FROM I CORINTHIANS 13

I have preached consistently and declared that **love** is the binding factor as we seek to properly relate to each other. Members from different backgrounds, varying nationalities, cultures, creed and preferences will come together as a local church. Therefore, love is essential. Let us review the points that I extracted from the "Love Chapter".

Careful consideration reveals that 1 Corinthians 13 is a complete treatise on Christian ethics and more so, it is an exposition on the philosophy of meaningful living. Three main points that I proffered in my previous studies as we studied the matter of love in the "Love Chapter", are as follows:

1. The Characteristics of Love (v. 4-7)
2. The Continuity of Love (v. 8-13)
3. The Clarification and/or the Conclusion concerning Love

I propose that one way to view all the characteristics listed in these verses of 1 Corinthians chapter 13 is to examine them separately under seven (7) headings that are all features of love namely, patience, kindness, generosity, modesty, unselfishness, purity of mind, and optimism. However, using the King James Version, and substituting the word "charity" for Love, let us take a closer look into this concept of love.

## The Characteristics of Love (v. 4-7)

Verse 4
"Charity suffereth long, and is kind; charity envieth not; charity vaunteth not itself, is not puffed up."

- Love *suffereth long*. Love is long-suffering, patient, long-tempered. It does not seek revenge. It is slow to anger.
- Love is *kind.* Love reacts with goodness to those who mistreat us, and is always in service for others.

- Love *envieth not.* Love is not jealous. Love does not bear envy in the heart.
- *Vaunteth not itself. Is not puffed up.* Love is not proud. Love does not parade itself, it is humble, and meek.

Verse 5
"Doth not behave itself unseemly, seeketh not her own, is not easily provoked, thinketh no evil;"

- Love *does not behave itself unseemly.* Love is not rude. Love is not arrogant. It is important to stress that the visible witness of the believer is what the world sees.
- Love *seeketh not her own.* This means that love is not selfish. Sharing and caring for each other is important, as shown in the model Early Church. All of them had all things common.
- Love *is not easily provoked.* Love does not fly into a rage. Love does not yield to provocation of any kind.
- Love *thinketh no evil.* Persons who love do not bear resentment. Love bears no malice.

Verse 6.
"Rejoiceth not in iniquity, but rejoiceth in the truth;"

- Love *rejoiceth not in iniquity*. Love cannot sympathize with evil actions. There is room for discipline within the body, but there should be no compromise with evil.
- Love *rejoiceth in the truth.* Two points that must be emphasized:
    (a) Love **LOVES** truth and (b) Love **IS** truth.

Verse 7.
"Beareth all things, believeth all things, hopeth all things, endureth all things."

- Love ***beareth all things.*** This characteristic is the same as "suffereth long".
- Love ***believeth all things.*** This entails giving a person the benefit of the doubt. It is close to the next feature – Hopeth all things.
- Love ***hopeth all things.*** Love trusts the best for all. Believeth and hopeth are linked. They may be summarized thus. "Because love believes, love hopes. Love has a future; love looks a long way ahead; love sees eternity."
- Love ***endureth all things.*** This is the same as long-suffering, and patience.

# The Continuity of Love (v 8-13)

[8]Charity never faileth: but whether there be prophecies, they shall fail; whether there be tongues, they shall cease; whether there be knowledge, it shall vanish away. [9]For we know in part, and we prophesy in part. [10]But when that which is perfect is come, then that which is in part shall be done away. [11]When I was a child, I spake as a child, I understood as a child, I thought as a child: but when I became a man, I put away childish things. [12]For now we see through a glass, darkly; but then face to face: now I know in part; but then shall I know even as also I am known. [13]And now abideth faith, hope, charity, these three; but the greatest of these is charity.

Love survives. Love is the summary of God's actions. Love never ends.

# The Clarification and/or the Conclusion Concerning Love

In my examination of this chapter on love, I have drawn attention to the opening verses of 1 Corinthians 13, which follow directly on the heels of Paul's correction of the "holier than thou" attitude of members of the Church of God in Corinth. In chapter 12, Paul corrects certain members who misunderstood spirituality. We see Paul correcting certain members who did not have a clue what spiritual maturity was. Verses 1 through 3 of chapter 13 finds Paul clarifying, and at the same time concluding as he emphasizes that the spiritual gifts and deeds manifested in the life of an individual fall short if there is no LOVE.

The deduction, then, my dear readers, is that if the individuals do not have the right relationships with each other, it is possible that such persons are mere members of the congregation, and not members of the Church. Members of the church know, and practice LOVE. Amen!

# Reflection

Pause for reflection, dear reader. How do you the individual measure up to these characteristics of 'agape' love? Evaluate yourself in relation to right relationships with each other. Consider your interpersonal relationships. How do you measure up? How does your church measure up in the display of love to each other?

# PART 3

# THE PEOPLE ENJOY A RIGHT RELATIONSHIP WITH THE COMMUNITY THEY SERVE

# CHAPTER 5

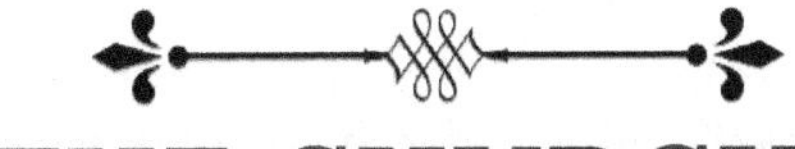

# THE CHURCH IN COMMUNITY

# The Witness

This witness of the Church in community is a public one. If the activities, the rationale, and purpose for the assembling together are conducted in secret and in closed quarters, then the public witness of the Church would be non-existent. The purpose of the gathering together is to share our experience of the good news of the Gospel of Jesus Christ. The disciples of the Early Church gathered themselves together, and something dynamic and miraculous happened. It was so spectacular that they could not keep it to themselves.

So, it ought to be today. When an individual experiences the change of heart that accompanies the salvation experience, and becomes converted, the hope is that this would be so impactful that he or she can hardly keep quiet about it. Some may wish to shout it out over the rooftops. Some desire to tell everyone they meet. This kind of news demands to be gossiped about to all and sundry to family, to friends, to work colleagues and in every public space. The Church individually and corporately should therefore publish God to the world in every sphere of our lives, and that IS the priority!

My pastoral ministry throughout the many years included service in developed cities, towns, and rural villages. While the public witness of the local church may have varied in consonance with the perceived needs of each community, I have found that there was usually very positive response to evangelistic and social outreach activities.

I recall one particular occasion in which the committed members lived in the inner-city community surrounding the church building. The needs of the community were being met by the local church in every sphere of life: from the babies at the Basic School, to the feeding of senior citizens. The weekly medical and dental clinics were offered free to the citizens, and the youths were engaged in sports clubs and leadership training. Individual entrepreneurs were also being assisted by the local church with machinery and instruments as needed. A community project was also developed to provide employment and necessary foodstuffs for the community.

The miracle of public witness arose out of this community project, when thieves from outside the area broke in and stole goods and equipment. On the morning after, I led a prayer meeting in the street outside the project building, and by four o'clock on that same afternoon, I received a telephone call in the church office, advising me to collect the equipment at an address in the community. The matter had been handled by the community members themselves without police involvement. The service provided to the community by that project was restored. The community members recognized the value of the project, the benefits to the community and the worth of the local church.

# What about Church Growth?

In keeping with the example set by our model church, when the congregation is the Church souls are *added daily* to the membership (v 41). This speaks to church growth, qualitatively as well as quantitatively. As members intentionally engage in right relationship with God, and with each other, spiritual maturity must result. Emphasis sometimes is often placed upon the qualitative aspect of church growth, leaving the numbers to follow unplanned. Church Growth is a significant marker to the effectiveness of the gospel message, and while I do not wish to address the matter of church growth in this book, it is important to address this from the perspective of evangelism, as people continue to enjoy right relationships with the community.

## The Impact

The impact of the local church means that the wider community must be impacted. In Acts 2 verse 47, the Church had *"Favor with all the people"*. For the sake of understanding, let us here consider the ministry of evangelism, and discuss how to develop a sustained program of evangelism in the local church.

Evangelism is "the spreading of the Christian gospel by public preaching or personal witness", as defined by the Oxford Dictionary. Evangelism may be further defined as the presenting of Jesus Christ, so that by the power of the Holy Spirit, persons come to put their trust in God through Him; to accept Him as their Savior from the guilt and power of Sin; to serve Him in the fellowship of the Church; and to follow Him in the vocations of the common life. It is a ministry of reconciliation, of humans restored to fellowship with God.

In the New Testament there are at least nine words are used to describe the evangelism that took place in the Early Church. Let us review them.

- *Marturĕō* – Sharing your experience with others (Acts 1:8)
- *Lalĕō* – Talking to others (Acts 4:1)
- *Ĕuaggĕlizō* – Telling others about Jesus (Acts 8:4)
- *Didaskō* – Teaching others the gospel systematically (Matthew 28:20)
- *Dialĕgōmai* – Answering reasonable objections (Acts 18:4)
- *Katagĕllō* – Driving home the gospel (Acts 17:3)
- *Kĕrussō* – Announcing the gospel so people can respond (Acts 8:5)
- *Mathateuō* – Convincing others to follow Jesus (Matthew 28:19)
- *Pĕithō* – Persuading those who are hesitant (2 Corinthians 5:11 & Acts 18:4)

Jesus' mandate or last command "to make disciples" (Matthew 28:19) should be the first concern of every Church ministry and individual Christian. The Church exists to convey to all people the message of Christ – Evangelism. The Church functions not only as the center of worship, Bible study, fellowship and social service, but as the center of evangelism with the membership and the clergy participating together in this great task. Evangelism fails when it becomes regarded as a special activity for special people at special times. It succeeds when it is regarded and executed as a normal activity for the entire Church all the time. Evangelism MUST be a regular and central part of the Church's activities.

The leadership of every local church should be directing the Church in a perennial program of evangelism. THE LEADERSHIP IS KEY. When the "passion for souls" grips the mind and heart of a Pastor thereby displaying in his/her own life and ministry a deep, genuine love for people, it ignites the fires of spontaneous evangelism, and the members will burn with like passion.

The following are possible approaches to evangelism within the local church. It is important to uphold, in a central place, the fact that *every approach must be bathed in prayer*.

# Evangelism Approaches

*Crusade Evangelism* – In this modality, the Gospel is preached to many in a focused effort, but the response is an individual and personal decision. The timing, location, and choice of evangelist is carefully planned.

*Friendship Evangelism* – This is when each member must do his or her part. However, those who would talk to their friends about their Christian faith have to be taught, and must seek to learn how to bring it into their conversation. This is also referred to as *Personal Evangelism*.

*Small Group Evangelism* (Cell Groups) – This modality is one of the most significant trends in the Church today, and needs careful, sensitive planning and organization. Remember that Jesus spent much of His time with individuals or small groups.

*Visitation Evangelism* - The Church is viewed as a training center out from which Christians leave, fully prepared to witness for Christ. This activity needs to be systematic, and must adopt an approach suitable for the community.

*Retreat and Camp Evangelism* – In a closed, unique environment, with focus on the individual, this approach appeals to many non-churched persons, and caters to new ideas.

*Open Air Evangelism* – This is a dynamic and vital modality to present the gospel, using a variety of methods (e. g. film, sketch board, PowerPoints, Large screen TV's). It also needs careful planning and execution.

*Vocational Evangelism* – This refers to evangelism with all its components of witness and invitation, reconciliation and sharing, in the turmoil of the world, and within the structures of the world. It is not so much a method as it is a broad undergirding base for all the various elements and facets of evangelism, and allows for being a witness wherever you are.

*Mass Communications Evangelism* – This method employs the use of literature, films, radio, television, and other social media platforms. Proper training is needed to carry out this type of evangelism.

## Points Regarding the Public Impact of the Church

Every auxiliary or department in the Church should be **evangelism-conscious,** and should make every effort to get its unconverted members to commit themselves to Christ; e.g. the Sunday School, Youth Fellowship, Men's Fellowship, Women's Fellowship and other groups or cells within the wider congregation. Each local Church needs to select the evangelism methods that are most suitable.

# Evangelism versus Social Concerns

The example of the Early Church outlines a logical step for each local church to consider as it relates to their relationship with the wider community and the socio-economic conditions of the persons they serve. The question of how to deal with poverty and the numerous other interrelated problems of our day has divided Christians into two camps. One builds a strong case for evangelism as the basic solution, while the other emphasizes direct social involvement.

In my early years of ministering in an inner-city community of Kingston, I felt the need to become heavily involved in providing for the members of the society, engaging in social activities to ensure the wellbeing and upkeep of all. As a result my projects and social activities drew the attention of a senior pastor in the community whose reprimand to me was that I was getting too involved in politics. I had used my contact and influence in securing needed materials, foodstuffs, startups for youth activities, care for the elderly, medical provision for those unable to afford it and many other projects which are too numerous to mention here. I was not an activist, nor was I a pietist in the true senses of the words, but I was chastised for my social involvement. Ignoring that, I continued to do what I was led to do despite the circumstances in my area of ministry.

There is a fracturing impact of polarized thinking that compels Christians to believe that they must be either *activists*, who attack entrenched social evils, or *pietists,* who emphasize the life of prayer, worship, devotion, and personal evangelism. Overcoming this is only achievable by the realization that both perspectives are important. Pietism and activism are interdependent. Pietism is the root of Christian life and activism is its fruit. Expressed in other words, a church that sets out to do the works of God, spreading into every area of life, yet neglecting the living center of belief, is doomed not to renewal, but to decay. The passion to do the works of God must be inspired and controlled by a stronger and deeper belief.[4]

A glimpse at the example of Jesus shows that He ministered to the whole person. See Luke 4 v 18-19; Luke 10 v 27 ff. Other Scriptures reveal this concern clearly, as in Galatians 6 v 10; Matthew 5 v 13-16; and 1 John 4 v 19. However, when "acts of love" are without the dissimulation of ulterior motives (such as being merely "bait" to win converts), the deeds of kindness are sermons even when no advertising "commercial" is attached to the specific act.

Expressions of love, in fact, any "love for others" that is merely "in the heart" without any outward expression is not love at all. True love always involves deeds, not just devotion; activity, not just attitudes; works, not just worship; facts, not just faith. (See 1 Corinthians 13 and James 2!). Any "love for souls" that neglects the physical body is a perversion seeking selfish rewards. The world is quick to see the inconsistencies of those who come with the words of a gospel of love but lack the support of loving deeds.

What then, is the recommendation? *Active Social Concern,* which is a concentrated study of the needs of the society and group dynamics in order to fill the perceived needs. An active social concern also can do much to promote evangelism. It demonstrates what love is so that people learn by example and by experience what is meant by the love of God; they cannot respond to verbal accounts of God's love if they do not know the operational definition of what love is. Social ministries remove the barriers of hunger, pain, anxiety, and other economic, physical, psychological, and social problems which otherwise prevent many people from truly hearing the gospel when the message of Christ is spoken to them. Christian social concern

---

[4] Moberg, David O. *The Great Reversal – Evangelism versus Social Concern.* Scripture Union, London, 1973.

plants and waters the seeds of the Gospel that in due time will yield their increase. As the Parable of the Seeds illustrates, some of the seeds fall on fertile ground and flourish well.

Active social concern thus promotes evangelism. Evangelism gives people new motivations, a new outlook on life, new self-concepts, and a new set of values that helps them to change their goals, their manner of living, and their social, economic, and political behavior. Dedicated attention to social concerns significantly contributes to the effectiveness of evangelism which simultaneously contributes to the implementation and fulfillment of social concerns.

Here are some focal points of Social Outreach that may be employed to strengthen the impact of the church on its wider community.

1.  *Social Outreach levels*

    (a) Personal level – individual making the effort
    (b) Community level – the church congregation planning opportunities to serve the community where they are located
    (c) National level – the church participating in social concerns run by the state
    (d) International level – involvement in outreach beyond national borders

2.  The involvement of Christians *in politics along with the matter of State and Church. This* point is crucial for Godly influence upon national decision-making.

On a personal note, as a representative of the church, I have found my involvement in national and civic societies to be extremely rewarding, as it reflects the moral rectitude and insightful decision-making that may be applied to matters of state. In serving on boards and national committees, I have sought to emphasize a divinely led aspect of the concerns being addressed. The respect shown, high regard usually expressed for my opinions and point of view have always made me grateful to God for those kinds of opportunities to share and participate at those levels.

# Reflection

Dear reader, as you reflect on your personal witnessing, please examine prayerfully, your commitment to this aspect of your Christian life and ministry. How do you measure up? Are there areas in which you believe you can improve?

# CHAPTER 6

# THE CHALLENGE

As I stated before in the first chapter of this book, the Church is more than a single denomination. The Church is not an improved Judaism. The Church represents the saved of all ages. The Church exists in two distinct versions in the Bible. Firstly, as the Universal Church, incorporating all who have been reborn of God and baptized into the Body of Christ. Secondly, as the local church inclusive of those in the Universal Church who have linked themselves together into a specific community of believers.

This community of believers ought to operate as a body, with all parts functioning and working together for the good of the local church and the Universal Church. The people have a right relationship with God, with each other, and with the community that they serve. This is when the congregation truly IS the Church. Over the last three years, this level of commitment has indeed been challenged by the COVID-19 global pandemic, where the Church has been forced to abandon the congregating together. I could not in all conscience fail to make this reference to the pandemic, because of the wonderful experiences in my own sphere of ministry.

The use of advancing technology has given us major opportunities to be creative in outreach, in Bible studies, in worship gatherings and even in evangelism activities. We are now literally forced to be innovative in caring for each other, and in sharing with those members who are unable to fend for themselves. New strategies compel us to learn how to use the various platforms to stay connected with each other. In fact my online Bible study and prayer meetings include participants from across the globe. Ministry activities are experiencing a new paradigm shift. The post-modern Church therefore needs to continue seeking and incorporating ways to remain geared to the times amidst the challenges.

# The Need for Appraisal and Action

So, as I conclude, there is need for appraisal and action as leaders and members assess whether they are part of a congregation or a church. The secular practice of performance appraisal on an annual basis is not regularly practiced within the Church. Leaders tend to shun the vulnerable position of being appraised by their members. Members, out of respect for the leadership, most times hesitate to indicate how they truly feel about their leaders and leadership methods.

My challenge to you, the reader, is that you would give yourself permission to engage in deep introspection regarding all the principles set forth in this book, and to use the two appendices included as a guide. The first one is to assist the leaders and members to appraise the congregation against the example of the Early Church in Acts 2 verses 37 through 47. The second Appendix is for the individual believer, church leader or member. Each individual is encouraged to stop and ask the Holy Spirit's guidance in shedding light on your own conduct, as you reflectively examine your own spiritual growth and maturity.

The effectiveness of this exercise in introspection will begin when you, the believer, the individual Christian, and the leader open your life to the full work of God's Spirit in a conscious act of the will. Reflection and analysis will produce spiritual growth for the individual as well as the congregation. Growth in the Spirit, called by some "progressive sanctification," will occur, and will produce an increasing awareness of oneness with God and effectiveness in Christian service. This is the true outworking of the Spirit-filled life! This is spiritual maturity. It is my fervent prayer that we all will continue to strive for the oneness, the unity, and true fellowship as we maintain right relationships with God, with each other, and with the communities in which we serve.

# APPENDIX 1

# APPRAISAL OF THE CONGREGATION

APPRAISAL-CONGREGATION: ______________________

Date of Appraisal: _________________________________

This appraisal instrument is *anonymous* and is intended as a self-appraisal for the individual member on the basis of three (3) characteristics of the Church described in the Scripture passage found in Acts 2: 37-47.

Please respond with a tick (√) in the relevant column indicating "Y" (for "Yes") "N" (for "No") or "?" (for "Uncertain/Don't Know"). Return the completed Appraisal to the Pastor.

## SECTION A: THE MEMBERS ENJOY A RIGHT RELATIONSHIP WITH GOD

| Criteria | Explanation | Text | Y | N | ? |
|---|---|---|---|---|---|
| The Conviction | The members are pricked in their heart and act upon the conviction of the Holy Spirit | V 37 | | | |
| The Explanation | The members are told the way of restoration to God | V 38-40 | | | |
| The Response to the Gospel | The members are obedient to the Gospel | V 41 | | | |
| The Baptism | The members appropriate the message and follow the Lord into watery Baptism | V 41 | | | |
| Holy Communion | The Members observe the ordinance of Lord's Supper | V 42 | | | |
| The Doctrine | The members continue faithfully in the study of the word and teachings of the church | V 42 | | | |
| The Fellowship | The members continue steadfastly in the fellowship, not forsaking the assembling of the saints | V 42 | | | |
| The Prayer Meetings | The Members continue steadfastly in Prayers | V 42 | | | |
| The Supernatural Element | The Members exhibit supernatural signs and wonders as they allow God to use them | V 42 | | | |
| Praises and Worship | The members fellowship with joy, praising God in unity | V 47 | | | |

## APPRAISAL – CONGREGATION
## SECTION B THE MEMBERS ENJOY A RIGHT RELATIONSHIP WITH EACH OTHER

| Criteria | Explanation | Text | Y | N | ? |
|---|---|---|---|---|---|
| The Recognition of the Leadership | The leaders are recognized appropriately in the church | V 37-47 | | | |
| The Caring and Sharing | The members share all things generously with those in need | V 44-46 | | | |
| The Oneness / Unity | The members continue with one accord in oneness and unity | V 46 | | | |

## SECTION C
## THE MEMBERS ENJOY RIGHT RELATIONSHIPS WITH THE COMMUNITY THAT THEY SERVE

| Criteria | Explanation | Text | Y | N | ? |
|---|---|---|---|---|---|
| The Witness | The membership is increased daily | V 41 | | | |
| The Impact | The members enjoy good relationship with all the people | V 47 | | | |
| Evangelism Outreach | The members participate actively in the evangelism thrusts | V47 | | | |
| The Supernatural | The community members see the signs and wonders and experience Godly fear | V 47 | | | |

## ANY OTHER COMMENTS / OBSERVATIONS

|  |
|---|
|  |
|  |
|  |
|  |

# APPENDIX 2

# APPRAISAL OF THE INDIVIDUAL MEMBER

## APPRAISAL-INDIVIDUAL ______________________________

## Date of Appraisal: ____________________________________

This appraisal instrument is *anonymous* and is intended as a self-appraisal for the individual member on the basis of three (3) characteristics of the Church described in the Scripture passage found in Acts 2: 37-47.

Please respond with a tick (√) in the relevant column indicating "Y" (for "Yes") "N" (for "No") or "?" (for "Uncertain/Don't Know"). Return the completed Appraisal to the Pastor.

### SECTION A:
### THE MEMBER ENJOYS A RIGHT RELATIONSHIP WITH GOD

| Criteria | Explanation | Text | Y | N | ? |
|---|---|---|---|---|---|
| The Conviction | I am pricked in my heart and I act upon the conviction of the Holy Spirit | V. 37 | | | |
| The Explanation | I hear about the way of restoration to God | V. 38-40 | | | |
| The Response to the Gospel | I am obedient to the Gospel | V. 41 | | | |
| The Baptism | I appropriate the message and follow the Lord into watery Baptism | V. 41 | | | |
| Holy Communion | I observe the ordinance of Lord's Supper | V. 42 | | | |
| The Doctrine | I continue faithfully in the study of the word and teachings of the church | V. 42 | | | |
| The Fellowship | I continue steadfastly in the fellowship, not forsaking the assembling of the saints | V. 42 | | | |
| The Prayer Meetings | I continue steadfastly in Prayers | V. 42 | | | |
| The Supernatural | I exhibit supernatural signs and wonders as I allow God to use me | V. 42 | | | |
| Praises and Worship | I fellowship with joy, praising God in unity | V. 47 | | | |

# APPRAISAL – INDIVIDUAL MEMBER

## Section B:
## The Member enjoys the right relationship with other

| Criteria | Explanation | Text | Y | N | ? |
|---|---|---|---|---|---|
| The Recognition of the Leadership | I recognize and respect my leaders | V 37-47 | | | |
| The Caring and Sharing | I share all things generously with those in need | V 44-46 | | | |
| The Oneness / Unity | I continue with one accord in oneness and unity | V 46 | | | |

## Section C:
## The Member enjoys the right relationship with the community

| Criteria | Explanation | Text | Y | N | ? |
|---|---|---|---|---|---|
| The Witness | I witness to others daily to increase the membership | V 41 | | | |
| The Impact | I enjoy good relationship with all the people | V 47 | | | |
| Evangelism Outreach | I participate actively in the evangelism thrusts | V47 | | | |
| The Supernatural | I exhibit miraculous signs and wonders so that the community may experience Godly fear | V 47 | | | |

## ANY OTHER COMMENTS

| |
|---|
| |
| |
| |
| |

# REFERENCES


Adams, Jay E., *Shepherding God's Flock: A Handbook on Pastoral Ministry. Counselling, and Leadership*. MI: Zondervan, 1986

Anglin, Lenworth. "Church Asked to Re-examine Purpose and Mission." *The Daily Gleaner*, March 28, 2008.

____________________."The Interaction between Culture and Worship." In *Let's Praise Him Again: An African Caribbean Perspective on Worship,* ed. Joel Edwards. Lottbridge Drove, Eastbourne, E Sussex: Kingsway Publications, 1992.

____________________. "Introducing the JUGC." Address to Media Conference held by Church Umbrella Group at the Jamaica Pegasus Kingston Hotel, Kingston, Jamaica on July 29, 2010.

Byrum, Russell R. Christian Theology: *A Systematic Statement of Christian Doctrine for the Use of Theological Students*. Anderson, IN: Gospel Trumpet Company, 1925.

Maynard-Reid, Pedrito U. *Diverse Worship: African-American, Caribbean & Hispanic Perspectives*. Downers Grove, Illinois: Intervarsity Press, 2000.

Morgenthaler, *Sally. Worship Evangelism: Inviting Unbelievers into the Presence of God*. Grand Rapids: Zondervan, 1999.

Moberg, David O. *The Great Reversal – Evangelism versus Social Concern*. Scripture Union, London, 1973.

Niebuhr, H. Richard. *Christ and Culture*. New York, NY: Harper & Row, 1975.

Ogden, Greg. *Unfinished Business: Returning the Ministry to the People of God*. Grand Rapids, MI: Zondervan, 2003.

Olson, Roger E. *The Mosaic of Christian Belief: Twenty Centuries of Unity & Diversity*. Downers Grove: Inter Varsity Press, 2002.

Rhodes, Stephen A. *Where the Nations Meet: Church in a Multi-Cultural World.* Downers Grove: Inter Varsity Press, 1998.

Saucy, Robert L. *The Church in God's Program*. Chicago, IL: Moody Press, 1972.

Smith, F.G. *What the Bible Teaches: A Systematic Presentation of the Fundamental Principles of Biblical Truth*. Anderson, IN: Warner Press, 1945.

Stafford, Gilbert W. *Church of God at the Crossroads*. Anderson, IN: Warner Press, 2000.

Stevens, R. Paul. *The Other Six Days: Vocation, Work, and Ministry in Biblical Perspectives*. Grand Rapids, MI: Wm. B. Eerdmans Publishing Company, 2000.

Stott, John. *Involvement: Being a Responsible Christian in a Non-Christian Society*. Vol. I. Old Tappan, NJ: Fleming H. Revell Company, 1985.

Tenney, Merrill C. ed. *Zondervan Pictorial Encyclopedia of the Bible.* Grand Rapids, MI: Zondervan Publishing House, 1977.

# About the Author

**Rev. Dr. Lenworth Newton Anglin, C.D., D.Min. D.D.**

Rev. Dr. Lenworth N. Anglin is the immediate past Executive Chairman of the Church of God in Jamaica and has served the Church of God Reformation Movement in various capacities, for over forty-five years in Jamaica. He also served the Church of God in the United Kingdom and was a pioneer member of the Jamaica Umbrella Groups of Churches (JUGC).

Rev. Dr. Anglin is currently giving Pastoral oversight to the Cavaliers Church of God in Jamaica in rural St. Andrew. In addition, Rev. Dr. Anglin is a widely used speaker at conferences, conventions and evangelistic crusades locally and overseas.

He is an honours graduate of the Jamaica Theological Seminary (JTS) where he is also a Member of the Board of Governors, and a part-time lecturer. He also chairs the Board of the Leadership Training Institute of the Church of God in Jamaica and lectures part-time.

Rev. Dr. Anglin earned a Doctor of Ministry Degree (DMin) from the Anderson University, School of Theology in Anderson, Indiana, USA. He was also later conferred with an honorary Doctor of Divinity (DD) from the Caribbean Graduate School of Theology (CGST) in Kingston, Jamaica.

Rev. Dr. Anglin's civic national involvement includes serving as the Chairman for the Governance Committee of Jamaica's National Partnership for a Prosperous Jamaica (PFPJ). He has received many awards, including the national honour of the Order of Distinction, Commander Rank (CD).

## Book Reviews

If you enjoyed this book and were impacted, send feedback to the author via email at hyalen@yahoo.com. Tell a friend and please write an honest review wherever you bought it online. Book reviews are the lifeblood of authors. It is social proof. Thank you.